I Know Directions

I KNOW
UP AND DOWN

T0004736

By Rosie Banks

Gareth Stevens
PUBLISHING

first
concepts

Directions tell us which way.

EXIT

3

Up and down
are directions.

5

I walk up.

7

I walk down.

8

The ride goes up.

11

The ride goes down.

13

The girl looks up.

15

The girl looks down.

17

The shark swims up.

19

The shark swims down.

We can go
up and down too!

23

Please visit our website, www.garethstevens.com. For a free color catalog of all our high-quality books, call toll free 1-800-542-2595 or fax 1-877-542-2596.

Library of Congress Cataloging-in-Publication Data
Names: Banks, Rosie, 1978- author.
Title: I know up and down / Rosie Banks.
Description: New York : Gareth Stevens Publishing, [2023] | Series: I know
   directions | Includes index.
Identifiers: LCCN 2022025539 (print) | LCCN 2022025540 (ebook) | ISBN
   9781538282977 (library binding) | ISBN 9781538282953 (paperback) | ISBN
   9781538282984 (ebook)
Subjects: LCSH: Orientation–Juvenile literature. | Polarity–Juvenile
   literature.
Classification: LCC BF299.O7 B366 2023 (print) | LCC BF299.O7 (ebook) |
   DDC 153.7/52–dc23/eng/20220715
LC record available at https://lccn.loc.gov/2022025539
LC ebook record available at https://lccn.loc.gov/2022025540

First Edition

Published in 2023 by
Gareth Stevens Publishing
2544 Clinton Street
Buffalo, NY 14224

Copyright © 2023 Gareth Stevens Publishing

Designer: Leslie Taylor
Editor: Therese Shea

Photo credits: Cover, p. 1 (stripes) Eky Studio/Shutterstock.com, p. 23 (image) Stanislaw Mikulski/
Shutterstock.com; p. 3 Rioji/Shutterstock.com; p. 5 Chonlatee42/Shutterstock.com; p. 7 MemoryMan/
Shutterstock.com; p. 9 Ekaterina Stepanova Photo/Shutterstock.com; p. 11 In The Light Photography/
Shutterstock.com; p. 13 VIAVAL TOURS/Shutterstock.com; p. 15 Dina Uretski/Shutterstock.com; p. 17
Kamira/Shutterstock.com; p. 19 Alexyz3d/Shutterstock.com; p. 21 Ken Kiefer/Shutterstock.com.

Printed in the United States of America

CPSIA compliance information: Batch #CWGS23: For further information contact Gareth Stevens at 1-800-542-2595.